The Bee Gees

A Little Golden Book® Biography

For all the Allen siblings, the big and the small. —K.A.

By Kari Allen
Illustrated by Leo Aquino

A GOLDEN BOOK • NEW YORK

Text copyright © 2023 by Kari Allen
Cover art and interior illustrations copyright © 2023 by Leo Aquino
All rights reserved. Published in the United States by Golden Books, an imprint of Random House Children's Books, a division of Penguin Random House LLC, 1745 Broadway, New York, NY 10019. Golden Books, A Golden Book, A Little Golden Book, the G colophon, and the distinctive gold spine are registered trademarks of Penguin Random House LLC.
rhcbooks.com
Educators and librarians, for a variety of teaching tools, visit us at RHTeachersLibrarians.com
Library of Congress Control Number: 2022942319
ISBN 978-0-593-64516-1 (trade) — ISBN 978-0-593-64517-8 (ebook)
Printed in the United States of America
10 9 8 7 6 5 4 3 2 1

Barry, Maurice, and Robin Gibb made up the pop-rock band the Bee Gees. They were singers. They were songwriters. They were disco icons. But most importantly, they were brothers.

Barry Gibb was born on September 1, 1946. His younger twin brothers, Maurice and Robin, were born on December 22, 1949. All three were born on the Isle of Man, an island between Ireland and England.

The brothers grew up with music all around them. Their father, Hugh, played the drums and was a bandleader. Their mother, Barbara, loved to sing. The Gibb family also included the boys' older sister, Lesley, and younger brother, Andy.

When Barry was nine, he was given a guitar as a gift. Shortly after that, Barry, Maurice, and Robin started performing around town. The brothers sang in harmony, which is when singers' voices blend together.

Back then, they called themselves the Rattlesnakes. The brothers were certain that one day, they would become famous.

In 1958, the family took a boat from England to Australia to start a new life. The brothers entertained the other passengers on the long journey.

In Australia, they played to crowds at a local racetrack, catching the attention of first a race car driver and then a DJ. Both had the same initials as Barry. Because of that coincidence, they renamed their group the BGs. Soon after, their name officially became the Bee Gees.

Nine years later, the brothers decided to return to England to chase their musical dreams. It was 1967, and the London music scene was hopping. Everyone loved a group called the Beatles. The Bee Gees hoped people would love their music, too.

The Bee Gees got to work writing and recording. They were inspired by legendary Black musicians such as Smokey Robinson and Otis Redding, who played blues and Motown music. The brothers worked those musical styles into their own songs.

Their first big single was called "New York Mining Disaster 1941." The brothers wrote this song in a stairwell during a power outage!

It was soon followed by two more hits, "To Love Somebody" and "Massachusetts." The band's first number one song in America, "How Can You Mend a Broken Heart," was released a few years later.

HOW CAN YOU MEND A BROKEN HEART

The band was doing great! But people's taste in music was changing.

The brothers needed to do something different to keep their fans interested. They went to Miami, Florida, to record their next album. Being in a new place inspired their new sound.

In the Miami recording studio, Barry sang falsetto—
which made his voice sound higher—and the band
used synthesizers to create a more electronic tone.
With these changes, the Bee Gees' new disco sound
was born!

The biggest hit from their new album was "Jive Talkin'." It quickly boogied its way up to number one on the music charts. The Bee Gees were back on top, and disco fever took over the world!

The Bee Gees' producer requested some new songs for a movie he was working on. Little did they know, this movie would make the band more popular than ever. *Saturday Night Fever* premiered in 1977. One of the band's most famous songs, "Stayin' Alive," played during the very first scene.

The *Saturday Night Fever* soundtrack didn't just have one hit written by the Bee Gees—it had seven! The album sold forty million copies and won four Grammy Awards. Disco was played in clubs around the world, and everyone danced to the Bee Gees' music.

1960s

1970s

The Bee Gees had hits in the 1960s, 1970s, 1980s, and 1990s! And with each decade, their style changed. Their hair was short, long, and shaggy. Their music was slow and fast. They sang low. They sang high. They sang together. And they wore everything from blazers to bell-bottom pants to sequined shirts.

But the one thing that never changed was their love of making music. When disco stopped being popular, the brothers wrote songs for other performers, including Barbra Streisand, Kenny Rogers, Dolly Parton, and Dionne Warwick.

After making music for more than forty years, the
Bee Gees were inducted into the Rock and Roll Hall of
Fame in 1997.

When Maurice passed away in 2003 and then Robin in 2012, Barry was left without his brothers. After thinking about their time together and their epic careers, Barry decided to make music again. He rerecorded some of the Bee Gees' classic songs with the help of famous country music stars like Keith Urban.

The Gibb brothers wrote over one thousand songs and had countless number one hits. Their harmonies are world famous, their lyrics tell stories, and their beats make people want to shimmy and sway. Their music continues to influence artists today.

The Bee Gees' sound is still **stayin' alive!**